In Praise of
Hispanic Sonnets

All of the poems in *Hispanic Sonnets* by Alex Z. Salinas can be categorized by intensity and precision. These poems utilize a ferocious language and challenge us to keep up with them in pace and idea. Somehow, the speakers become more and more clever with each poem. Maybe because, like Salinas himself, these speakers can conjure dreams from the wind, from the landscape around them, and from the many familiar people inhabiting these poems. As a Latino poet, I've long struggled with my ethnic identity while writing and have stared at the word "Hispanic" on the page and considered exactly what it means and how it relates to me. Salinas goes a long way in these poems to help us understand his relationship to this word and idea. In "Hispanic sonnet, or Dark heart," Salinas writes: "I'm like a split path casting dual shadows./ Like a shadow I'm a branch of my name./ I'm merely a name like everybody else./ Like everybody else I'm a collection of veins." In another poem, "Hispanic sonnet," he further explores his relationship to his culture and writes: "Mob movies are to Scorsese what taquerias are to me." Alex Z. Salinas, like the rest of us, is doing his best to define himself by ever changing and obtuse terms. Fortunately for us, Salinas has the language, insight, and tenacity to bring these ideas to life.

—**Aaron Rudolph**, author of *The Sombrero Galaxy*

In *Hispanic Sonnets*, Salinas reimagines the sonnet and creates an intricate collage of Dairy Queens, pop culture references, and Chipster literary ancestors. This collection is a vivid portrait of a

South Texas poet and the artists and places that haunt their dreams. *Hispanic Sonnets* is best read with abundant coffee and muted Spurs highlights playing in the background.

—**Cloud Delfina Cardona**, author of *What Remains*

Catholicism and skepticism during the pandemic linger through as the poet survives to write.

Salinas takes you deep into his memory, dream world and daily reality all mixed in with a hot cup of coffee. His poetry breathes political commentary and humanity in the time of COVID-19. An "ice cream date with Harper Lee at Dairy Queen" charms the reader and "You can beat The Lone Ranger but/ You can't beat Tim Duncan" is a range that raises fists in the air.

In *Hispanic Sonnets,* poet Alex Salinas delivers whip-smart haikus, thought-provoking couplets and inventive sonnets with a fling of a fist.

—**Vincent Cooper**, author of *Zarzamora: Poetry of Survival*

Hispanic

Sonnets

FLOWERSONG
PRESS

Alex Z. Salinas

FLOWERSONG
PRESS

FlowerSong Press
Copyright © 2023 by Alex Z. Salinas
ISBN: 978-1-953447-22-7

Published by FlowerSong Press
in the United States of America.
www.flowersongpress.com

Cover Design by Alex Z. Salinas
Author Photo by Jennifer R. Lloyd
Set in Adobe Garamond Pro

NOTICE: SCHOOLS AND BUSINESSES
FlowerSong Press offers copies of this book at quantity
discount with bulk purchase for educational, business, or sales
promotional use. For information, please email the Publisher at
info@flowersongpress.com.

Acknowledgements

As It Ought To Be Magazine: "Auditorium," "Overboard"

The Beatnik Cowboy: "Ars poetica as a fry cook named Lars Moetica," "Closet anarchist," "Drift"

Catch the Next Journal of Ideas and Pedagogy: "Hispanic sonnet, or Tongue-tied"

Cuento Magazine: "Haiku on San Antonio small talk in the age of COVID-19," "Haiku, or The art of letting go"

Dissident Voice: "Hispanic sonnet, or White names"

Dumpster Fire Press: "Hispanic sonnet, or Invisible wire," "Hispanic sonnet, or The burbs," "Raft"

Fevers of the Mind: "Essay on poetry"

Gnashing Teeth Publishing: "Bellyache, or Damn-fine meal," "Blender"

It Takes All Kinds: "Medieval motif"

petrichor: "Library," "Oh, y'know, just your standard Q&A," "Split"

Pioneertown: "Billboard"

Punk Noir Magazine: "Hispanic sonnet, or Punk sensibility"

The Rye Whiskey Review: "The keys"

San Antonio Review: "Resurrection"

Tilted House Review: "Blue Ye"

Yellow Mama Webzine: "Hispanic sonnet, or End of American maniac"

Table of Contents

I: I DON'T WANT TO CHANGE YOUR MIND, I WANNA STEAL YOUR HEART

II: TIMEOUT

III: HISPANIC SONNETS

For my brothers & sister & Beauty.

Every existing poem is a lie, ...

—Ben Lerner

A Note on *Hispanic Sonnets*

What is a Hispanic sonnet? It is a 15-line, free-verse poem with a separated last line as its own stanza. Each Hispanic sonnet's second and final stanza—that lonely little manmade island—serves as its volta, or turn, meaning that where the poem ends in idea, tone, or spirit is not necessarily where it begins.

Let it be known, then: a Hispanic sonnet is not really a sonnet.

Shakespeare transformed the 14-line English sonnet. Petrarch perfected the much-older 14-line Italian sonnet. Wanda Coleman dazzled with her rule-busting, 14-line American sonnets, and Terrance Hayes carried her tradition to new heights.

Corpus Christi's first Poet Laureate, Alan Berecka, informed me that writers he'd encountered have penned 15-line sonnets called quince sonnets. Having never attended a quinceañera or a quinceañero, I—a non-Spanish-speaking South Texan—smiled upon learning this grain of poetry's organic history—always adaptable to the influences of culture. Quince sonnets seemed to me, naturally, inevitable. The sweetest, tangiest apples and oranges ever within reach.

The poet Iliana Rocha, with whom I had the pleasure to read on a virtual open mic, has authored a beautiful, 18-line (by my count) poem titled "Mexican American Sonnet." Juan Felipe Herrera, former United States Poet Laureate and the first Hispanic appointed to that role, once told me he'd removed commas from a poem after having mastered them.

It is in this shadow, perhaps, that I arrived at the unruly Hispanic sonnet, whose name is the only invention herein I claim. The chasm between two stanzas representing everything and nothing—the worst and best of what we are capable of in community and in solitude.

Everything else remains an inevitability.

Hispanic Sonnets

I

I Don't Want to Change Your Mind, I Wanna Steal Your Heart

Audacity

As soon as I conclude this stanza
I'm gonna wow you

As soon as I polish off my coffee
My words will fill their frames

As soon as I catch a flying image
I'll swing a mirror upon its body

As soon as I remember what to say
I'll jot it down promptly

As soon as I ... as soon as I
Rise from this deluge

I bang my head on the ceiling
As soon as I bandage my petite cortex

I dispose of peeling clichés
As soon as I incinerate mutinous sentences

I daydream of
Caressing cracked lenses through which I peep

As soon as I stop scratching my wounds
I lotion them with cream

As soon as I recite the Hail Mary
My bed swallows me

As soon as I brush my teeth
My teeth brush their teeth

I fantasize obliterating you with ruthless poetry
As soon as after this dot.

Burial

No sum of lashing will
Whip my tongue in shape

No drone of chanting will
Resuscitate wasted cockroach

From the ground up
Cockroach as Sphinx

From the Sphinx up
Pimpled ceiling as constellation

Did the poet choose couplets
Or couplets choose the poet

It took me 31 years to wear
Air Force Ones in all terrain

The closer I arrive to die
The chiller I feel inside

The Basquiat head hanging above my
Flatscreen stares me down hard

You never really hear on the news
Black-on-brown crime, which is

To say—we hate what we think
What they think we're not

I'll dignify Sphinx by encasing
Him in three Brawny sheets

Entombed Sphinx as Ozymandias
IKEA trashbin as Valley of the Kings.

Haiku on San Antonio small talk in the age of COVID-19

They don't know nothing.
Leave it to God. Hey, what time's
H-E-B open?

Billboard

SERIOUS INJURY? on a billboard screams across
The clouded sky
Clouded sky screams through Adam Smith's
Megaphone
Adam Smith's megaphone threatens the promise of
Death
Death promising every day
Every day Death the banker
The Banker in his shiny blue suit
A man isn't made of much if
His suit shines, my grandfather said
Grandfather favored a denim jacket in his
Final days
Left me his jacket, which doesn't fit
Many things don't fit anymore
Time leaves me ill-suited
Checked my tongue this morning to see if
Español still lacks
But your master's in English, señor, it reminded
And English Literature, I nearly corrected
Today I bought Hemingway's
Death in the Afternoon at a
Used bookstore
I don't feel used one bit
Feeling and fact aren't the same, I heard Grandfather say
"I don't believe in ghosts," I spat back
Except this poem lolls upon the dead

Here's how you trap ghosts in 3 easy steps:
    Shut eyes
    Picture hate / love
    Embrace
At the gas pump earlier, the screen yakked at me
Reality vaguely disappointed
Returned home to find my tank less than empty
Only then did work begin
Marveling at birds screaming across
The beautifully clouded sky.

Call to action

Before my grandfather slipped away from the living
With a rosary wrapped around his long hands
I was to become a lawyer.
He'd arranged for me to meet people in secret cantinas.
There was too much money to earn.

Now that he's been gone
I want nothing to do with the long arm of the law.
I find qualities to admire in people I meet
But I prefer to keep away from them.
There's too little to earn in poetry.

Ask my pen if it cares.

Motorcycle

I dreamt I knew the day my grandfather would die
Even though he was already dead
And he told me how on the day his grandfather died
His legs burned like an engine and so
He hopped on his motorcycle and never looked back—
He was already dead when he taught me how to drive
And he said, Smash the rearview mirror with this—
A beautifully tattered copy of *Don Quixote*
In the velvet tongue of our brutal fathers
And he said, Capture your woman with this—
A sterling silver rosary turned black from
Oil, greed and time
And he said, Become friends with the judge with this—
A bundle of cash wrapped in Sunday comics
And he said, Keep your woman forever with this—
A pacemaker plucked from his shriveled core
And I drove down I-10 alone
With engine roaring like a hellbent angel
And celebrated each passing mile by
Tearing a page of *Quixote* and feeding it to the vultures
Even though the vultures were gone and the sun was a dream—
It was just me and my bad heart in a denim jacket
And I said, Go a little bit faster, it's alright,
No policemen will stop us here.

Pipe bomb

I dreamt I was a pipe bomb in a
Pipe dream and I was nobody. My
Hunger was gone and I was nothing.
I chased my tail out the door and
Called it waltz and from out my heart
Burst Mozart. Then the ghost called
Shakespeare clogged the well with
Brick folios I couldn't understand with
Eyes sunk and forsaken like a mattress
In Death's backyard. I was a stick
In the mud called Literature for the Deaf &
Blind and my purpose was nothing except as
Lightning rod for the gods. I was
Happy—all pieces & no mind and electrolytes.
Any century now the fire would swallow
My fuse and how the denizens danced so
Much prettier than me. How the rain
Cleansed our feet without bloody permission.
Really, that was the least of our worries.
How bliss thrived under each of our beds.
Soft. Firm. Spring-coffin rhythm & blues.
Arresting songs. Distractions. Names
Echoed until melted into shadows.

Judgy

I dreamt a coffee-stained book of
Ernest Hemingway short stories
Featuring his mug on the cover hacked
Right through my soul, as if such a thing
Were probable, & for a few outlandish
Moments couldn't determine if I was
The one judging the book by its cover
Or if the book was weighing my heart's
Merit, breaching its chambers & finding no-
Thing inside but a tatty teddy bear, as if
Hearts were bred in the toy factories of
Books—a fate I'd never considered—thus
I lost my composure & swiped Papa's
Pompous likeness off the table, to which he
Then peered at me from the ground up, his
Illusive gaze none the wiser—or rather,
Sizably hardened—then I thought,
At least you're not wearing a skirt, boyo
(As if the option weren't already on the table).

Ode to the high schooler reading Foucault at Barnes & Noble café

Congratulations
I can't judge your
Pedestrian taste in pop lit
Just your endeavoring to
Skirt the bell curve
Your iced coffee looks smooth
I hate iced coffee's stinking guts
I realize you may be
A freshman philosophy major
Congratulations
Insanity in the Age of Reason
Birth of the Prison
Archeology of Knowledge
Oh yes
Heavens no
I'm listening …
You seem like a good kid
Your stylishly messy mop
Foucault would've agreed with
The part about your hair
When I was your age I was reading
Nobody
I should stop babbling
Thinking that is
When a poem is self-righteous
Somewhere in France a baby chokes on tears
It's bad luck to harm children in art
But there's no bad in art
Only preference

And you're no child
Justin Bieber lookalike
Foucault bandwagoner at Barnes & Noble café
This poem's acting perverse
Begs me to tell you something imperative:
Foucault sounds like *fool's gold*
Chopped at the knees
Kneecapping (don't google it)
The Order of Things is such that
There are many things to
Order before we up & poof
Up & poof would be a majestic way to exit the scene
And yet you're already gone.

Proper noun

I dreamt the Alamo's
Front doors were spray-
Painted with white words:
South Texas is hell—
And the good Catholic in
Me capitalized the *h*.

June buggin' out

Found a crushed June bug in my patent leather
Boot then mourned missing mothers

Hilarious I scan things and
Map phantom father-lovers

If children were lawmen or ball
Players / who'd spin lacquered fibs?

Once I scaled a dying oak tree / launched
Cracked my budding ribs

I loot unspeakable projections rare as ruby mint
Sizzling cinnamon'll do, thank you

Craving sunrise Sunday two-handed pray
Though sweat glands sobbing "ew"

If children were poets & lawbreakers
I'm doomed to sweep cleaving streets

When rivers jog dry / moat throats too
Christmas cajoling mum caked in cadaver sheets.

Nov. 3, 2020

Cover font of
John Coltrane's
Stardust looking
Western—
"Southwest Art Deco"
Clarified m'lady
& we belted
Giggles cuz
Specificity cracks
Our bubbly guts
& I wonder if
Stars gauge the
Optics of
Their visage,
Ponder the
Nova of their
Affairs—
Do they
Blush & swell
Upon knowledge of
Final burst?
Wish upon their
Twinkling bodies
As we pray
To tonight's
Eyeballs tallying
Executive votes?
There's an

Orange peel
Barricaded in
Oval Office—
Banana peels
Lie in wait.

Drift

I dreamt the king had died &
Come to life &
Upon a throne of warped records
Kurt Cobain growled
My girl, my girl, don't lie to me
Tell me where did you sleep
Last night
And up the tar-stitched avenue
Goethe dished dogeared copies of
Faust & frenzied
Citizenry wailed
O beautiful for spacious skies
For amber waves of pain
And Cobain rifled out his
Powder-coated brains &
Heavy rains reminded one of
Fables of invincible Old Glory &
Upon front-door rafts drifted we—
Survivors, naysayers,
Stayers of stale philosophy—
And a new wet world resurfaced O
So blue, O so green & in my
Prayers I answered the question of
The bygone musician whose needled
Passion soared always toward
Emptiness between stars:
Last night I slept in the kingdom &
Tonight, I learn to swim.

Instructions to a king

after Ishmael Reed

Do not carry a woman's belongings
For reasons concerning honor.
Do not label yourself king
And begin to understand your reign
As a birth certificate ripped in two.
An old novel instructs a tale
But doesn't rinse the blood
Off your sword, under your nails.
The skyrise doesn't care if you impale
Your legend on it. Your soles
Hold the sins of the country
Rich in color & smell. God
Will not save you—
The coming trial
Your tongue
Quenching none of your nation.
I've carved love hard unto others
And no one cried your name.
Ask yourself: Does my crown
Cut the sky behind which our dead dance
With angels? Does my skin
Stitch the wounds of outlived epic poems?
No. Trot daily & jot dreams into diaries.
Burn the pages & share your bread
Like shards of heartbreak subject to gossip.
Let them talk. Let 'em bond. If you are de-
Throned, you're a verb, a sliced wrist,

More or less. Hero & mirror, more & less.
You taste worse than you look,
Look worse than you sound. Dangling
Cigarette. Let us in & watch us fly
Off the cliff
One by
One.

Snowflake

Wake up
Reasonably intact
Something missing
Set you apart

Locate flower
Kneel beside it, sniff
Flap imaginary wings & say
"Zzzzzzzzzz" (be bee)

Stand stiff, no chatter
Flagpole—raise arms
Crucifixion staring
Contest w/ the sun (pretty juniper)

Lie down on dirt, no, sand
Flesh beach towel, discarded raft
Tell lewd lies supine like a
Corpse if the dead could speak

Face bathroom mirror, Narcissus
Tell yourself the gods are stories
That you'll emerge into Otherness a
Newborn if you headbutt glass

Cover left ear, postulant van Gogh
Plug both canals, transcribe notes
Headstrong Beethoven scowling at
Jupiter's final leaden bolt

Grip Bowie knife
Carve snowflake on abs
Call 911 (psycho-amateur tattoo
Artist bleeding through new shirt)

Snowflake engraved on
Snowflake yields narrow socio-
Political footprint, what
Critics call one-dimensional

Who wants kids anymore? Nobody—
Not entirely true, the world missing
From my hands, only lines suggesting
Palms signifying cordless crystal balls.

Telegrams

I have a thing for
Cheerful lips &
Drooping eyes as
I am the double of
All mirrors

What you see
I see a glimpse of

Who I wish to be
You see a peep of

My misaligned teeth
Are straighter than I think,
People say kindly

Telegrams of the soul is
Poetry, proclaimed
Richard Brautigan

What's more poetic than
Crooked smiles?

… poems about
Crooked smiles

A friend once asked:
"How do you write
Funny things?"

27

I replied:
"Be born funny"

In my case:
Coneheaded &
Jaundiced

A lover once asked:
"How do you write
Beautifully?"

I replied:
"Be born ugly"

In my case:
Coneheaded &
Jaundiced

I read once that
Good poems say
Everything

Which means
Mediocre poems say
Something

… about everything

Or possibly nothing

I hate choosing sides
Hate warming benches
Hate mowing lawns

I was born 50 years old,
My pops claims

Somebody should invent a
Game called Baggage Claim
Wherein players play bingo
On boards of assorted traumas

What's that supposed to mean?

Is outstanding poetry sorta
Mean-spirited often-
Times?

Spirit of '76

Who still subscribes to
The New York Times?

… Me
Digitally—
$4.26 a month, baby

Back then, I made peanuts
Now:
Walnuts

So fancy
So clever
Solidly adult

I can't stand when
People say "adulting"

Yes, I'm that guy—
The one born age 50

A friend once joked:
"You have your Boomer moments"

I nearly clowned back:
"Boomerang"

Fortunately for folks
I'm slow on the draw

Southern drawl like white gravy

As I lay dying
With spiders in my mind
The plumpest calls himself
William Faulkner whom I find
2 wily for his
Own good—
His sentences & syntax nonetheless
Magnificent train wrecks

Circling back on it
I'm not the double of
All mirrors

Barely even am I the untraceable I in me

¡Ay yi yi!
It's 1:12 in the morning

Pardon me while I stretch this
Thing like plastic wrap on a CD—

No return policy

Best Buy, Sam Goody

Salinas, we're trapped in the
Past

Claw our way out
But with what chewed-up nails?

Resume remarkable boredom

This has to wrap up sometime
… has to close shop eventually

The ink well's drying so
Sleep well

Goodnight

Sweet dreamzzz.

Haiku, or The art of letting go

Drove my haikus to
School, drove home, counted to 10—
They grow up so fast.

Blue Ye

I dreamt I cracked open the
Skull of Kanye West &
Found unnamable jewels the
Color of Prussian blue &
A tin voice purred to me
Follow God
And in the news I was
Celebrated not as grave-
Robber but Indiana Jones of
Hip-hop boneyards which
Marked me a target among
Thieves of raiders & my
Indigo precious stones were
Auctioned as priceless & the
News eschewed my deed &
Over the passage of 808
Heartbreaks my mind flung
Its dignity into Davy Jones'
Locker & a tin voice purred
We slithered into an unearthly world &
We're the cleanup crew.

Portrait of a portrait of the artist as a young man (for sale)

Hang it sideways, say double metaphor & gimme my money.

Stardust

Trane flows in 4/4 time

Eyes locked in distance, she says,

"You hear something the first time

Only once"

I, trained in old ways, leave her untouched

Solo she cries, 4/4 tempo

Toes tap carpet

Air cascades notes

Space Trane steals my love

The record slows

Stylus suspended

Sax bleeds on

Thy bent knees I kiss & squeeze as neighbor.

Stream of life

I dreamt I kissed Clarice Lispector—
That wistful, indecipherable Brazilian—
On the forehead &
She smiled as the hour sank the sun behind a
Flank of cigarette clouds.

Ghosted

I dreamt I was on an ice cream date with
Harper Lee at Dairy Queen & said, "I tackled
To Kill a Bald Eagle in ninth grade & gushed
At every page," to which Harper Lee snorted
And her Blizzard dribbled out her nose as though
She'd sneezed & in a way she did & once I had
Her giggling my jokes didn't cease until the
End when I said something to the tune of,
"American justice wouldn't be futile if folks
Just followed the rules," & Nelle, scooping
The last of her Blizzard, responded, *Without
Corruption & brutality, the novel would be toast,
No contest—thank you for paying for me,* & then
I drove her home & to my utter bewilderment she
Never answered my phone calls & later—but not
Soon enough—I forgot her face until 2015 when
Go Set a Watchman was published & upon finishing
The book, which was both sequel & prequel, I felt all
Over again, like a recovered nightmare, an unsettling
Song from the past, I'd zero clue who she'd been.

Red neon

I dreamt of a wall bathed in crimson from
A neon bulb & the moon cleansed itself
In our star's blood—it was '13 again
Because the promise of future clung to
My skin like an unforgettable lover's
Perfume before the ivory tower &
Raymond Carver & Junot Díaz would
Recruit me for the Army of Suffering
Scribes of the Void—I hadn't yet gained
The world because my body was still mine,
My mind & will were still mine, & all
Roads still led to happiness (not Rome)
And immortality was still a biblical
Eventuality & I had yet to commit to print
A solitary symbol I believed in—I was still
Satisfied by my byline on cheap newspaper
Stamped with cheap words I deployed by
The pound to potty train a puppy I never
Wanted but who I loved with all my cheap
Soul—love seemed so easy to find & so
Easy to buy & so easy to groom & rekindle
And regenerate as if time worked in our favor,
On our behalf for our gain & good graces to
Retain—under the radiant bulb like blood, like
Strawberry guts, like a personal invitation from
The red-light district, you asked what's the point of
Slaving away if not to make spectacular money,
If not to avoid ending up exactly like our folks

Counting every single penny, & I said:
Baby, you know you can't take that stuff with you,
And you said:
Neither can you with all your love in the world,
And I hated you—we fucked for what felt like
The final time & long after I stopped seeing the future
In you I acknowledged with courage & horror
That I was wrong about just about everything—
But I was already off in a foreign land fighting for truth
Vicious & beautiful (like a *sleepwalking warrior*)
And I wrote to you that I didn't think I'd return home
Anytime soon.

Roses

after Kaveh Akbar

Roses are red.
Roses are red especially dead.
Roses are rainbows sans everything but red.
I prick my fingers on roses.
My fingers gush hues of roses.
When I ingest sulfa my body breaks out in roses.
In the name of roses stalwart English tore off heads.
Umberto Eco smeared conspiracies in the name of roses.
Certain babies are photographed on beds of roses.
Certain babies are crowned after roses.
Apolo Ohno's soul patch is a garden of baby roses.
My mother's middle name is the singular of roses.
My mother allows only one to present her with roses.
Valentine's Day is slang for roses.
Roses is lingo for plague.
Love the smell of roses in the morning.
OutKast said roses really smell like poo-poo-oo.
I place petals of roses in the middle of unread books.
Rosy cheeks aren't as breathtaking as roses.
Rosacea is a disgraceful homage to roses.
The first buds I likely befriended in school: roses.
Licked a few roses in my days.
When my ghost says sayonara,
I'll bring a bouquet of 15 roses for Peter at the gates.

Medieval motif

after Tomas Tranströmer

Father and son sit across from one another on the sofa
Separated by a square board.

This is their first game, or the fifth.

The father, who sips gold he'd poured into
An ice-cold glass,
Had recently taught his son the rules of engagement.

The boy, now grown,
Remembers his father playing in an oil-stained uniform reeking of
Milk, although he actually wore pajama bottoms & a cutoff T,
Showered and face freshly foamed.

The boy—a man—hasn't a clue who claimed victory,
Although the notion is preposterous & beside the point.

It doesn't matter if the moon was full.

The man is certain he's battled his father for
The last time
With the sky on fire as witness.

Yet, at any time,
Even with mountains of sand in his mind,
The match proceeds
Whenever he wishes.

Stiffing

I dreamt I was third-wheeling a
Brunch date between Mark Twain
And Zadie Smith & was oddly
Threatened by Mark Twain's
'stache—that is, the lip caterpillar of
Samuel Clemens—so I told him,
"Your work is no longer time-
Less, just timely," to which Mr.
Clemens-Twain golf-clapped my
Slight & Zadie Smith rolled her
Blazing eyes into her beguiling
Head wrap—blood red in color if
Not sentiment—& then & there I
Knew I was the lone child at the
Adults' table with merely two slim,
Largely unread poetry collections to
My name, as if that were the Great
Divider of my life—& it was, it really
Really was, so without tipping, I left.

Ars poetica trifling

Contrary to binding logic
    Accretion of
Enchanted oxygen
    Accident jiffies enflame
Lustrous aortas
    Cherubic arrhythmias quelling
Embryonic tears—
    Lovely weather, my darling?
Sho' 'nuff
    Get this reckless burst
Outta sight.

Ars poetica truffling

Give or take
There are 360
Dog breeds panting
Our air

Only one
Lagotto Romagnolo
Is bred to
Hunt truffles

Before He
Winked the cosmos
There was
Word

Word was
With God
Word was
God

Word split
Bloodshot seas
Mongrel legionnaires
Christ punctured

This poem is
Too informal
Too mythic
Unripe

Word killed
The good boy
Who snuffed the
Last truffle

What came
First? Word
Or the ruined
Flesh?

Ars poetica as shadorma, or Vicious cycle

You're like me
and know every warm
poet has
one less heart-
beat. Deduct this from my time-
sheet. From yours. All love.

Ars poetica as a fry cook named Lars Moetica

Lars Moetica's father before
He perished from prostate cancer
Always told his malleable son
Son, all you have is your name

Lars Moetica these days can
Be found in late-night
Commercialized dungeons
Where corn oil is emperor

Lars Moetica accepted his
First paycheck as a fatherless
Child, invested in a chest tattoo:
All you have is your name

It's said Lars Moetica is
On the path to promotion
Only a scant year after his
Mustache penciled in

Lars Moetica is built to last
In the late-night dungeons
And he'll forever remain
Rail-thin

Lars Moetica takes to his
Name like a suicidal poet to
Conception pain—the words,
They never come out right

Lars Moetica will still somehow
Outlast his tag and still somehow
Float hemispheres & still somehow
Words nibble the relics of words.

Essay on poetry

for Robert Aaron Salinas

Little Brother
I know you didn't ask for an
Essay on poetry
But the mouse in my pantry
Needs exterminating
And we won't do it—
Mom raised us with clean hands if nothing else—
Great poets would strain to describe that fur of
Protruding gray,
A color that, like poetry, becomes the
Word & little else—
You didn't ask to sleep on my
Inherited couch, that velvet Panzer, trooper,
But Pops gave us a broad back if nothing else—
Things will start to change soon,
I feel it in my verse
Which is to say
A career balancing the innards of my skull
And when you send your pieces to review
I judge them not by punctuation or clarity
But rather how related our creature is
In a different house of bones—
Little Brother
The right lines are hard to come by
If one reads incessantly with sharpened preferences
And this game of penchants isn't for everyone
But the next time you visit

When 2017 is a faint dream
I promise you'll fall asleep on brand-new cushions
For a bed of roses cuts it only on the page.

Homework

I dreamt I had a homework assignment
Due yesterday, today, tomorrow, the day
After & each day forever—it was called
Being A Writer, gift from the Logos, a spell
Damned hypnotizing when sentences flowed
Right—& Nico Walker, freed man, liberated
Author, PTSD-lifer—whose tortured face sung
To life when I looked at it—patted my shoulder
And said, *Me too, brother, me too.*

Raft

Craft

Raft

Drifting

Sink

Only stay quiet while my mind remembers

The beauty of fire from the beauty of embers

John Masefield

As read by F. Scott Fitzgerald

Is it possible poetry died then?

Cardiac arrest—stroke of midnight

Me, a babe in a league of ghouls

"Gh": ghastly start for English words

Give it to ghosts, too

Especially those refusing to give themselves up

Craft is a raft,

In other words (a phrase my dead professor detested)

Poet, hast thee memorized poems lately?

Can thee perform thy scribblings well?

The raft is disappearing

Tugged into a horizon where the world hungers

Take it back

Poetry dies with me tonight

This city, embers watching through fog.

The keys

Came close last night to
Making words mean
Other than what they mean—
What do words mean beyond
Meaning?—beyond meaning
What do words do? What words
Do what & when do they
What? Do words when when they
What & why do they do what they
Do? Say what?
How do words mean & why
Do I care?
Where the flip are my keys?
"Where you left them," replies I.
I dig The Black Keys primarily
Because of their name.
What's in a name, a wordy funky name?
How many names can I stuff in the garage?
However many I want.
O how I wish to be what I
Can't & why God gave me
Poetry to write home about
I don't want to know why.
Beyond meaning, words are taffy—
The sponsored dessert of the
Parareal parallel to the
Ultrareal wrapped in surreal quilts
Knit by phantasms
Shoving me out the door

Onto the wending concrete
Into the glimmering skyscrapers of death—
Yes,
My keys were always in my hand.

Communion

I dreamt Cormac McCarthy
Dreamt the story of God
The story of God warpaint
God only a story
The mountains were real
The dirt real
Desert gyrating like heated gypsies
Stamped trails in the wasteland
Poundings of a thousand generations
A brown woman sat upon a horse unmentioned
In any volume
God handeth her manna
God only a story
A queue of darkened faces
Hostcupped hands
One swollen tongue by one
Woman placed seed
The queue heatdancing in the mirage
Crying & hosannaing
Old children of Mexico
The pale mare's mystical crest
The naked rider unburnt
Clipped of wings.

Resurrection

I dreamt I was the ashes of
Christ kneaded into Earth's
Folds proceeding the Ensuing
Flood, reanimated into Geoffrey
Chaucer's parched scrolls
Telling exalted tales of
Lustful knights & wily
Witches stretched tight
Into rouged skins of
Fair ladies, but soon
God's flames scorched me
Evermore, resurrected me a
Son of middling ilk, a ranch
Ghost milking cows, gawking at
Jade pastures, dreaming of
Pious Christian wives who'd
Someday under sherbet skies
Etch their likenesses in the drying
Family tree etched on the tattered
Inside cover of my faithful edge-gilded
King James bible.

Closet anarchist

The spines are rising on my shelves
And I can't fathom the eyestrain
Vacuuming complete cooled texts,
Refrigerated voices sealed between covers

If literature reaps lasting brain
Damage then I'm a pseudo masochist
And still the stacks swell as engorged lovers
And still my spine pinches toward Earth

This is the trail of a closet anarchist—
Sip your brew and to yourself flex
Time in which you honor your birth,
Your mother, books who bleach yourselves.

Closet antichrist

What's cooler than being cool?
Inquired rapperbruh André 3000
Ask the closet antichrist whose chief vice
Is never being a favored sunnuva gun

Sure can bend ears, boi, like Munchausen
Tho don't dispute his scriptural wisdom
Spurts defensive and throaty like a Detroit piston
Cooler than cool is wearing scapegoat's skin

If I told you the herein ruffian's name, well damn
Fukk all & roll your nice ivory dice
I crave boundless payday, turkey-stuffing sin
André 3000—man, your inquiry's ice cold, ~~fool~~ fam.

Library

I dreamt of a library in which
In the middle of an antechamber
Juan Rulfo sat reading a slender book—
Likely a long-forgotten poetry collection—
And I said to him, "Juan, Mr. Rulfo,
What the hell're you doing in here?"
I thought they weren't letting anyone in,
He replied. *I thought this palace was barricaded.*
"Sir," I said, "you calling me a ghost?"
He shut his book & smiled—
His pallid lips slitted like a corpse's.
He reached inside his blazer,
Pulled out a sepia photograph.
A picture of the sky, he said.
I call this "El Dios."
"You're crazy," I told Juan Rulfo,
"You must be a Mexican writer."
Then I gave him my email address,
Said to stay in touch, that I'd teach
Pedro Paramo to my students.
He waved me off & said,
Minor work by a minor visionary.
"You're nuts," I told Juan Rulfo,
"Absolutely mad. You must be the
God of Latin America."
I left & he returned to his book,
Peaceful, legs crossed like a gentleman.

City o' books

I dreamt I slept in a feminist bookstore in a city comprised
entirely of bookshops (but no libraries) & no matter the weather
the sunsets always cast a golden shine upon wood, brick & metal,
& the people—mostly transients, surely—said strange things like
"Remember when we were old?" & "This town of theirs where
dreams go to live" & not once did I witness a soul eat or drink
anything edible and on Day 2 of my stay a tall woman asked what
I was writing—a story, I answered—& she requested I read aloud
the first line to which I agreed—"Suddenly the phone rang, and
I knew it was Destiny calling"—& she said "Ah, yes, I know how
this one ends" & it was as though I was digesting an anchor that
was sinking me slow & I heard a report on the radio announcing
that in this town you'd be lucky to reach 65, that the risk of
perpetual subversive pleasure was—is—premature death—stroke,
suicide & the like—but the joys, O the glorious benefits & I
scrapped my predictable drivel in a wastebasket under a golden
sunset in the metropolis where everyone so casually consumed
ideas that I conjured not for the first time the visage of the bell
curve—so disturbing as to be sensual—in this city not mine
where it was a crime to hock loogies on books but not dogear
their pages & I recall a bookshop specializing in 19th century
tomes where it was said in the basement there was a morgue
where the dead consumed pulped magazines and Cuban cigars
but I've always been one for entrancing folklore & just as soon
an idea for a poem self-imploded in my head as I recalled the tall
dark-skinned woman who knew how everything concluded &

in my desolation it remained true that every word was the sperm
& every delicate page the egg & this incessant coupling we had
to thank for the true crime bookstores & Christian bookstores
& Latin American horror bookstores & bookstores for gamers
who abhor books & bookstores for the manga-blinded on every
corner & in every alley of this construction whose visitors—for
we are all visitors, my friend—passed the hours so delightfully as
to be their own exquisite tragedy & on Day 3 I saw a man with
salt-&-pepper hair & steely eyes—he looked like a Jack—who
slit two holes in his Bible so he could spy on unsuspecting bodies
like he was the centrifugal victor of his own drama & I was fixing
to walk over & hock a loogie on Ol' Jack's vandalizing face when
Mario Vargas Llosa & Anne Rice arm-in-arm called me from a
distance—they were smiling—their teeth impossibly bright—
their voice as one—*Hey, isn't this the most ridiculous place you've
ever seen, like childhood on a loop except you will at some point go off
the rails?—hey, come join us for a stroll!—we're looking for our works
so we can buy 'em all, every single last godforsaken copy!*—& that's
how I learned life's a traveling circus—a traveling theater without
walls—in which steaks & peanuts amounted to the same goop w/
proper lighting & cosmic perspective.

Oh, y'know, just your standard Q&A

1) **Do I exact revenge on blank spaces with machinegun words?**

> *You do not often take the high road with your art.*

2) **Do I connect the happenings of my inner circle with cosmic memory?**

> *You burn inside and spew with intellectual impatience.*

3) **Do I love every book I buy?**

> *You pray to treat all your children the same.*

4) **Does my olive skin belie what's frozen in photographs?**

> *You read faces as patchy sentences on serrated pages.*

5) **Do I run in ovals only to return to every place I know?**

> *I'm afraid so, my son, I'm afraid so.*

6) **Do I fear the underlying principles of the biological imperative?**

> *You heard today a kindergartener felt neither like a boy or girl but a rose.*

7) **Does the aftertaste of shopping malls plague me with buyer's remorse?**

You are accustomed to writing other peoples' stories in your voice.

8) **Does calling someone racist assuage our fear of the unknown?**

You figured out how to turn "off" daylight saving time on your G-Shock watch.

9) **Do I think I can hit the center of my truth with an abundance of years?**

You dreamt the silver cross you purchased in Hawaii was back around your neck.

10) **Does authentic beauty elude the tendrils of linguistics?**

You want to answer yes *but that might be a lie.*

11) **Do I still believe in my childhood hero?**

You'll go your remaining days trying to define the meaning of "honor."

Split

I dreamt my eyes were split wide
Apart—wider even than Julio Cortázar's,
As though in preparation for rainwater
To carve down my face a river, or perhaps
For it to lay as a landing strip for illegal
Aerial activity—midnight Cessna runs—
And my eyes on the sides of my head
Saw that I wrote in dual dimensions,
Right & Left, therefore I could no
Longer be a middling poet, I simply
Couldn't, as if my eyes (forked far & wide)
Had ruptured something inside me, some-
Thing intangible, irreparable, & my words
Would always blossom from concurrent
Divergent paths, paths destined never to
Lick each other, simple as that, & I cussed
The wretched force who wrenched apart
My eyes, spread them like butter, & was it
Cortázar's voice I discerned from my book-
Shelf? A smoky bass vibration that greeted:
Welcome, tiger, to the ongoing revolution—
How're your new eyes treating you?
To which I replied, "It feels like I only go
Backwards, to quote Tame Impala," to which
Cortázar, tickled, re-replied, *You youngsters baffle me.*

Colombian blend

I dreamt I turned my back on literature,
All the signs present, the writing
Withered, the last rejection paperweighted
By a stone of dust & Gabriel García Márquez
Hollered from the surface of my black coffee—
What some call the liquid grooming mirror—
Only a fascist pig thinks he's beyond himself
And I looked down at him, his bristly mustache—
Which is to say my next trim long awaited
Me—& to myself below I said, fatalistically,
"My knees are crumbling and my belly is acid
And my groin plummets and my mind is madness"
And Márquez grinned broadly at his twin the way
Only a Nobel Prize winner can & purely by chance
And real magic we spoke in unison, harmonically:
This dream, this dream, it's the only demise for me.

Auditorium

I dreamt I was invited to Vladimir Nabokov's
Auditorium to read some poems & impart
One piece of advice to his advanced English
Students—as in, they all possessed diverse
British accents—& I was jittery, butterflies in
My stomach, my face oleaginous (an adjective
My geology professor friend once used to de-
Scribe that vampiric doofus Ted Cruz) & upon
Conclusion of my reading, Nabokov cleared his
Throat as if to say, *Now onto the business about*
The 1 piece of advice, Salinas, & all I could
Muster in all my oleaginous splendor was,
"People suckle on doom & gloom's teat less
Pleasurably than you think"—less so advice &
More so self-help spewed into a mirror,
Refracted as a monochrome rainbow—to
Which Nabokov's students stood & clapped
Thunderously, whistled, wanted more, begged
"Encore! Encore!" & it was clear I was finally
Accepted by academia, I'd punctured the dubious
Membrane of the ivory tower, & then I glanced at
Nabokov who sipped from a bottle of Diet Coke,
The flesh around his eyes slack & bored, an un-
Tended mausoleum sculpted from an iceberg.

Overboard

I dreamt I was pushed over the edge
Before I was ready to jump
And the surface stung like a jellyfish's caress
As I sunk in the pusher's tears—
Herman Melville's agony—
And anchored to my ankle was
Moby-Dick
And I gurgled the ocean with a fleeting sense of
Poetic justice
As the cold watery locker
Reclaimed my lungs &
The sun sailed & vanished—
Would it dive in &
Resurface my aching bones?—
How was I to know?
A killer poet (& poet killer)
Was on the loose
And a line by Renata Adler
Rattled my suffocating mind:
Lonely people see
Double entendres everywhere—
Would Melville attend my estate sale
And buy my library wholesale?—
How was I to know?
The deep salty palace believes not in
Reinvention
But I don't pretend to
Speak for the darkness
Accepting me blindly—

Blithely—
Which is to say
Here I'm treasured
Even though I arrived by way of
Sitting on a powder keg—
Then I woke up & choked on my spit.

This is not an open letter to God

I want to
Give you
Everything

But when one
Bad meal renders me
In the fetal position

All of
Poetry
Is lost

Lateral on my
Sofa, my book spines appear
Like military ribbons

I keep reading them,
Stacking them
Somehow

I don't suspect
I'll find
What I seek

If my demons are
Angels in disguise,
Do I pass the exam?

God, we're a
Poor judgment away
From dirt

This is not an
Open letter to
God

When I'm gone
I wish my children to
Play my records

Though not once have I
Heard the ones my
Godmother left me.

Bellyache, or Damn-fine meal

One day
I'll run out of love poems
And the buildings will bend
Like praying knees

Heaven
Less than a messy dream

Maybe a kiss from God
Means something
To a buried child

To the earth
Hugging her so

The most alive person I know
Is dead & my old poem says
We laughed during our last meal

Imagine:
Our teeth like pebbles
Coffee-stained &
Anything but the stars

We spat in the face of
Death—
Wanted strangers
To applaud the diss

Memories like stories
Like words scattered like debris

Dry mouths made of the sea
Where I learned the breaststroke
Shortly after my full name

What's more human
Than seeing ourselves
Drown?

What's drowning
To the fish
In the belly of the beast?

Ethics of all I know

Woke up intoning the line
"The ethical storyline stretches from
Africa to Alabama"
And the dull ache of my
Big-toe hangnail
Begged to life &
I thought
Something's always there
Till it joins the stars
Like my godmother did that
First August morning
And they too flee the party—
Disappearing act—
The ethics of all I know
To think I once believed
Fallen raindrops lost
Planets rather than
Wet disappointments from
Unknowable
God.

10-part rumination, or Translucent whales

I.

When Steve Carell questions Paul Dano
In *Little Miss Sunshine* if he's taking a
Vow of silence because of Friedrich
Nietzsche, he's really saying: Silent films
Are Hollywood's most translucent whales

II.

I watched *Little Miss Sunshine* for the first
Time one month shy of age 32, having returned
The DVD to Hollywood Video 14 years ago
Because my father once declared his home an
Anti-viewing sanctuary from Rated R films

III.

When my lover asked if I liked the movie—
She'd purchased it for me via Amazon—I said,
"It was really good, it would've meant more to
Me when I was 18," especially the part when the
Family steals the grandpa's sheet-wrapped remains

IV.

I saw an old woman at Gold's Gym with a mestiza
Face, a body seemingly too fit for her age & the first
Thing I thought was, She looks like she belongs in a
Gabriel García Márquez novel, she's a Buendía &
Tonight she might plague the inside of my eyelids

75

V.

On Mother's Day at Dairy Queen the cashier was a
Maestro, his black ponytail whipping side to side in the
Spirit of spinning ice cream, his eyes alert & kind, his
Mouth cruel, his voice somewhere between servile &
Annoyed, which made everything come together

VI.

In Fredericksburg I slept in a motel room plastered with
Posters exclusively of John Wayne & not once did I com-
Plain or contemplate desecrating the property which is
More than I can say for the Duke whose Christian name,
Mind you, is Marion Robert Morrison—square like a jaw

VII.

I'm currently tackling Valeria Luiselli's *Faces in the Crowd*
And someplace in the novel she writes as Gilberto Owen
And women who script as men & vice versa net my reader-
Ship—on another note I'm 4 pages deep into *Moby-Dick*
And someday (I swear) I'll devour every American classic

VIII.

The truth is I adored everything about the motel room in
Fredericksburg, call it the curse of Enchanted Rock, call it
Country living, call it two spiders tucked in the bathroom
Corner forging war, making love, producing silk & generally
Speaking staying out of my way but hardly out of sight

IX.

Generally speaking, I'm quite greasy these days, my hair is
Whitening & running away, an irresponsible & contrary fate

Compared to my books, which inch toward my roof & soon
A vengeful fire will consume them, it's true—these days
I pen about flames constantly & yet my toes still feel cold

X.

I dreamt I told my bosses to go to hell & lost my job &
Awoke to the absurdity of chuckling—or was it barking dogs
That smothered my brain in reality?—then I watered my mini
Madagascar palm—I call him Planty—reminded myself my
Best me flourishes in shaded, highly pressurized spaces.

2 startlings + 1 full disclosure

Last year I was on the
Can reading a debut
Novel by a Mexican
Writer (a compliment
In my mind) & sipped
Pike Place® & placed the
Cup on the countertop &
The emerald siren's smiling
Face denoting an empire
Suddenly startled me.

I flipped on the faucet to
Purify my mitts & out
Sputtered water & the
Rude noise startled me &
I muttered, "Jesus effing
Christ," though in this re-
Telling I'm overly prudent
Not spelling out the middle
Obscenity as it had been
Exhaled with utter ease.

I lied—the aforementioned
Events transpired today &
So my sins resume tallying
Till my finale, though if you
Think about it the dead in
Their external expansion

Commit loads of crimes that
Keep detectives detecting &
Loved ones behind weeping,
Frankly, at the strangest times.

Pigeon

There are so many birds flying so often
All week my eyes see one thing
A screen
      But there are so many birds
Flying high
In trees
      Some sing
I saw a pigeon fly today
My head buzzed beautifully
Uneasily distracted
I'm too accustomed to weary
It isn't that there are too many things outside to see
But outside there are too many things
      The birds
      Breath mints of Easter
I don't know them as well as I think
Every month I hike
Unkindly into my body
Regret mossing beside time
Today I saw a pigeon fly
      Pitied it and me
Tomorrow must bring what it brings
But today   a pigeon flew through me.

A little help from my friends*

We're like two ships drifting apart
at sea

What you underwent is a small death
preparing you for the Big Death

Cool beans—no, beans should be warm

I'm not sure I truly understand but
the imagery is beautiful

I think I will keep track of how many
times he uses the labyrinth metaphor

Who says, Oh, I'm feeling kinda
lackadaisical (?)

Someone's gotta give ya crap every
now and then

Listen—you are creating a written
time capsule and future generations
will think of us the way we think of
the word "yuppie"

Her parents are so much bigger than
her it's funny

Dang dude—did you really try to
force yourself to vomit?

81

That one felt like a punch to the
stomach & all too familiar

It's so wild, right? They're just one
huge, fetid mass

I assumed all men love Butterfinger

To be honest it's completely
autobiographical

I love pigeons they're such
underrated birds

Warp speed

I hope you survived this winter storm

Y'know, I think "jovial" is exclusively
for Santa

Those painted?

In general our language is trending toward
immediacy, so this could help make the
past tense more active—cut all the
passive backstory

You think batter and abuse are
inevitable?

Holy crap, I thought I was the one on
the dark side

Yeah that's a level of commitment I
just can't reach

There's always an ulterior motive

Our former president has the lizard-
brain skill of manipulating the zeitgeist,
the American attention span

I'm on medication again but the
fact that life is meaningless is
usually at the front of my head

I can still function, nothing serious

Or develop a chronic state of hypoxia

Imposter

I am grounded and currently feeling the
importance of maintaining this
earthly body

Damn covid

Maybe leave that out of the article

Do your magic

Time is like the arrow that always
and never reaches its destination

Similarly, I've not heard from your
editor, to whom I sent a critique of the
mag, overwhelmingly positive, of course

Give your first novel one more chance to
express itself if only to croak an additional
minor syllable or two—you'll be
happy you did

I'll give you a Roger Ebert review in
the next few days on your new book

I'll bring my copy—I want a
nonsensical note inscribed

I read the poems—Mike said it was a
walk down childhood memory lane

Some of the poems in your volume seemed
so very Texas to me in ways I found
unpleasant

What is the perfect story? It's the
one that isn't written because it
can't be written, because it
lives in our memories
only

Too often your art does hurt
(a reader like me—not the poet)
but it does so without taking
necessary voyages

Learn and work and be honest

I'm pleased you've discovered the books
and I hope you'll persist with them all

(though of course they're quite different—
it's unlikely you'll be pleased by every
last one…)

I wonder if all these books and my others
feel as though they're in a station waiting
for a train that will never come

I'm not sure what binds all these
together but they seem to share an
ecosystem.

* *The author accepts full responsibility for two of the above stanzas.*
For artistic and historical (read: nostalgic) purposes, the remaining he
seized from confidential companions.

Poem for Spurs fans

An old woman entered the café
With skin like a damaged saddle
And sky-blue South Texas eyes
Lost to reason long ago.

She repeated this loud like a psalm:

"You can beat the Lone Ranger but
You can't beat Tim Duncan."

A few of us raised our fists.

Fingerpaint

I cannot sterilize the humor in the horror
Nor should I—I, who spent my youth
With a blond-haired, blue-eyed best friend
And who wished upon a blue genie to turn
My surname into Smith, only to be greeted
In Spanish yesterday by Indians managing the
Valero, a rare occurrence but still—
Their welcoming, I mean, in our irresponsible
Country where my brown-skinned childhood hero—
My godfather—glorified Trump's MAGA-red crusade
While telling me how decades of working at the
Milk plant broke his bones beyond repair—
The irony, I'm aware—how my father laughed off
The existence of the mustachioed Frito Bandito,
How his dark glare seems to judge other strangers as
Thieves—for good reason, I repeat like gospel—
How in one family the American Dream
Becomes drawn & quartered, how in one body
Time extinguishes countless passions
Leaving behind cicada shells of obscure lines
From battered books and flopped films—
I dreamt of a wedding band that fit our nation's
Fragile fingers but not the whole world's—
Perhaps when I'm older I'll write a poem for my
Child about how when I was their age I despised
Fingerpaint and how now I desire little more than
To stain whitewalls with purple palms as if to
Proclaim: *Here is where I am & here's where I remain.*

Drying streams

Equal chance of
Unlikeliness
The tissue of horrors
(What Baudelaire dubbed the press)
Knows of what it leaks
As poets avenge close to
Sense
On tissues of horror as
Chika Sagawa—
Whose stomach failed her in '36—
Finely expressed that
Night is already in my hands,
Crack eggs & out spills the
Moon
And spiral into
Excision on a
Screen of horror
Knowing well the quixotic
Quest sprung in Spain—
Half my history's highland—
And drowns here
Somewhere
In the drying streams of
My blood.

Beautiful world

Listen—the world's not beautiful.
The people would have you revolve
Around a set of unclear parameters.
The world's bounty its blue blur,
Constant chase of bloody crimes—
The world's a lonely hunter
And we its fleas—a huge infestation
We know takes only one
To bring this beast to its knobby
Knees. Wrap the rosary round my wrist
And what about my itchy neck? My
Red eye died on someone else's watch.
Sunday, midday, sun's out—every-
Where I look a plaza of encounters
Ensconced in a warm pool
Inches shy of real touch. For how
Can we trust the cracked mask
When the phantom's escaped thru the
Back alley like a gangrenous fold
Of some foe thought vanquished
In the gassed trenches of my mind?
In the center of the plaza, a smile so
White like a star in the country darkness.
A ghost in the glow-black of city night
Where a million loves overshoot the moon
And never learn the meaning of family.
Keep your guard down—but is that how
The heart keeps pumping? Oftentimes

The literature misinstructs. Close the book—
Crawl toward the obvious choice. Show me
Everything I think I know. Then show me
The mirror beneath your fragrant clothes.
I promise to act quite surprised. Promise
Not to frighten you with ungodly wishes
Which are little more than shadows cast
By dried leaves—tombstone dash between
Falling & fallen. Brief lives cut into stone.
Cold-lesson roads carrying me home
Down the throat of tomorrow.

Angel baby

When you are near me, my heart skips a beat
I can hardly stand on my own two feet
— Rosie and the Originals

Light an apple
On fire
No timer
The roast
Your heart.

I walk through your heart

I walk through your heart
Filled with rooms of
Halls of mirrors
And when I feel disgusted
With myself as is oft true
I watch my legs kick off
Like the man on the moon
Who knows he's free
And dies alone
With sweltering lips
In space so vast
He can't thrust his way out—
Is it worth it?
You ask from the other side—
"Wouldn't change a thing"
The reflection answers
Like a glowing morning
Keeping the cloak of night away.

Blender

As in dreams, as in life, in steaming black coffee
The faces fade, the bodies fade, heat fades

She critiqued Bolaño's books saying they lean
Toward self-destruction & she was right

"Everything points to death," she said
And then I kissed her soft white neck

I slept sleepless for a week straight &
Thought, If I go away for a good while

The voices in my head become colorless
As if time is the Great Blender

I remember drinks my mother used to shake
Slush the color of tapioca, or was it lime green?

I dreamt of becoming tall like my maternal grandfather
And he was the first to enter back into the dirt

I think of how Dante dreamt of Virgil
And how I daydream of Bolaño's dangling

Cigarette saluting the ground on which he trampled
My dirt, his dirt, the earth of Latin America

I'm not Latin American—not American
I'm the color wedged between two maps.

Like a spring breeze

We will all die.
We are monsters in the dark.
Killers in the light
Carving love hard into our beds.
In others' eyes
We see how little
Is passed in a kiss.
(Like a spring breeze.)
The times we say we will not let go.
How resolute
Is the release.
Yesterday is only a story.
Tomorrow is only a word.
My body only a sheet.
"Revision is erasure"
I pray to the sky
Piggybacking the universe so to speak.
So what do I do?
I burn the sheet.
I live in the ashes of my poem
Which doesn't exist.
Not a Goddamn thing alters the stars tonight.
This is how my brutal god prefers it.
We mistake *saved* for *freed*.
I will die rearranging them.
Their meanings sink me. (I think.)
I sing into the Void
Which rips apart my name &
Conceals it in a thousand unread books.

On one end of the library: paradise—the other side: hell.
I have spoken only for myself.
Allow me to carouse the aisles for as long as I please
And when I lose you (I always do)
I reinvent your smile again and again
Which I carry inside my chest alongside death.
The best years I have spent.
The worst hurt earned.

I wasn't born on the Fourth of July

But the red on the flag is my blood.
My mother's lipstick the evening of her wedding.
Brilliant bursting rockets flooding the fly-studded air.
Equality & immortality making jokes
Of whipped tongues.
I declare: Dish out your heart
Like little pieces of expensive pie
As if in possession of flawless credit
The balance of which carries into the afterlife.
Entrenched roots.
Extraordinarily American.
Rhyme & shining reason skipping hand in hand
Through plank-trapdoors
Beyond which pain-faced angels sing our names.
Buzzing phones.
Operatic rebirths.
The green pastoral sea filled with mighty adversaries.
All ye who answer server-fried ads
Please be braver than me.
Let us praise the fallen leaves on my welcome mat.
Let us hock loogies on unoriginal book covers.
Let us bury our animality with currency.
Let us pacify crying children on balconies.
Let us solve the problem of we, the progeny of infinity.
Let us call a broken bus a dusty shoebox.
Let us dry our bodies with dignified Old Glory.
Let us resurrect Gatsby's *old sport*.
Let us capture our identity on the other side of the mirror.
Let us confound intelligent masses
With profoundly imbecilic poetry.

Let us bow over Gutenberg's grave.
Let us swallow the ashes of history's flames
And confess our transgressions to the bloodless moon.
I wasn't born on the Fourth of July
Must be why I hate apple pie.
I considered destroying this document as if it never existed.
How many more times can I change my mind?

I don't know if the truth will set you free, but resolvability is for the birds

And the truth is

Death is not resolvable

The swaying trees, the blades of grass

Leaves in the breeze all along

If I last

My answer is

You didn't adore them enough.

American sonnet, or Squeaky clean

I stain tiles above my tub; I'm a credit to my kind
I stain tiles above my tub; I'm a credit to my kind
I stain tiles above my tub; I'm a credit to my kind
I stain tiles above my tub; I'm a credit to my kind
I stain tiles above my tub; I'm a credit to my kind
I stain tiles above my tub; I'm a credit to my kind
I stain tiles above my tub; I'm a credit to my kind
I stain tiles above my tub; I'm a credit to my kind
I stain tiles above my tub; I'm a credit to my kind
I stain tiles above my tub; I'm a credit to my kind
I stain tiles above my tub; I'm a credit to my kind
I stain tiles above my tub; I'm a credit to my kind
I stain tiles above my tub; I'm a credit to my kind
Hiring to scrub above my tub; afraid who I'll find.

II

Timeout

The ruinous recognition that (probably) next week, next month, next year, end of watch, (certainly) a billion centuries from today, nobody will have read you, remembered you, you're not even an illusion, dash of molecules, quark in a fading galaxy, tinier than that, wisp of poetry long evaporated, & so to soothe your nerves—reignite an impetus for work—you shower, hot water prying open your pores (you're present now—here, you're alive) & like a plea bargain you grasp for straws, compromise, so-called middle ground

III

Hispanic Sonnets

Hispanic sonnet

Was ashamed of my culture
Am a credit to my kind
Culture translates to food & language
Food & language translate to every Mob movie
Mob movies are to Scorsese what taquerias are to me
Which is to say the entanglement is uber complicated
Übermensch is a noun that sounds cooler than it is
At 17 years old I fashioned myself an Übermensch
My pops didn't learn his first name till he was 5
He & I are penalties of appropriation
You are a product of appropriation
We are products
Ever fancied yourself an unfinishable project?
If our incessant projections manifested as laser beams

The world would be the dopest light show in the world.

Hispanic sonnet, or Prodigal son

Could be Jesus' Parable of the Prodigal Son
Isn't a story of forgiveness, but battery.
Sons must always spurn their fathers.
I'm convinced El Greco knew the score.
He left his land & leapt into eternality,
Fathering a son who wrecked in later years.
It took my father four decades to let his body
Be filled with the breath of God.
It took me 372 months to face the mirror &
Clasp my cheeks as long-lost relatives.
I love my brothers & sister as my limbs—
Some days they glide as gracefully as breeze.
I'd define my affiliation with cemeteries as
Awkward & bittersweet.

Someday my skin'll slide off & I might be free.

Hispanic sonnet, or Wimp Icarus

My maternal grandfather once ascended so
High in his Cessna over Mount Rushmore he
Spat globs of whiskied phlegm on skullcaps of
Four rocky all-star prezes & the globs hardened to
Stones & so too do words upon fleshy impact
Sting like pellets indifferent to mortal plights.
The flight—would you hate me if I confessed
This story's made up? Not the Cessna part nor
The sorta-sortie across the colossus. It was more
Cinematic than that. I promised myself ages ago
I'd enroll in aviation school once I earned my
Master's degree. Look at me—still no wings. Still
Me. I'm Icarus minus divine drive. Or maybe my
Wings were clipped wombside, which is so Greek

Tragedy—me, mercurial inveigler, crying shame.

Hispanic sonnet, or Guidance from a U.S. Poet Laureate

The illest poet of these mighty fine States
Once advised me to master the tongue then
"Get rid of that punctuation" as if that were
Literature's most pedestrian resolution & that
Blistering recommendation scrambled my wits
Like eggs & I'm reminded of a bold classmate
Who referred to Shakespeare as Billy Shakes &
The time he stood & defied antiquated lectures on
The finer points of Othello's *thick lips* & informed
Our soon-to-be retired professor that everyone in the
The boxing ring—his second home—gets labeled a n—
And well, we all cringed, although I was brought back
To the blacktops where I too was once called that laden
Fabrication as though somebody was screaming at me

In the heat of competition: Brother, get back on defense.

Hispanic sonnet, or Apologist

Halting production on my novel-in-decline
To write that if you view late-night
Shows upside down, the hosts' grins are
Frowns. The audience erupts at dud
Jokes & the talent is on the verge of hysteria.
When news rang of the ancient blue president-
Elect, I, driving down I-35, told my cousin that
The only positive trait of the crazed leader of
The free world is eternal optimism. My cousin
Nodded collegially then said Heath Ledger's
Performance as Joker better explained
Humans than anything he'd seen during his brief
Spooky stint as paramedic. He's dark that way,
My cousin—resting on reckless actors' laurels.

We place premiums on the squandered & wicked.

Hispanic sonnet, or Vanilla Oreo

Trane, you, with your big ol'
Fine sax abducted my gurl & I
Want her back—you've rendered
Me a child, a putto, a baroque
Tantrum who corrodes in rain.
Quick tangent: I've never smooched
A lover with a tongue ring though
I anticipate the experience to be
Something between heaven &
Heavens no-coming-back-from-
That. I'm terribly silly tonight.
Terribly willy-nilly—like a tongue
Ring wrapped in leopard print.
Ay, dios mio, I'm too detached from

Abuelita culture. Puro Vanilla Oreo.

Hispanic sonnet, or Gridlock

Two ageless warlocks are in gridlocks
On my tongue.
Geographically they're mobile & march
The path of least resistance.
Like water. Like language.
My middle name's an amalgamation of
Roman occupation & the varied ways
Peoples of Spain mouthed their
Brutish sovereign.
The warlocks wage battles that may
Never be won.
I'll die with their ruins
On my tongue.
A mandible split down the middle.

Upon death, tongues bulge swollen with pride.

Hispanic sonnet, or Gettin' old

Woke up with a pain in my shoulder blade
And was reminded I know my body like
I know myself, which is to say, as an
Acquaintance & not very well. Today
The sky's a sheet of concrete. The hanging
Leaves eye the ground. My first thought—
I, ever the poet—was, Alejandra Pizarnik
Would be happy right now. A flash of
Glee in an Argentine life terrorized by
The implication of poetry, of words that
Must only lead to finales. Though she
Overdosed in 1972, Pizarnik bears
Striking resemblance to a former editor of
Mine from back in my newspaper daze.

Ibuprofen expired, I swallow my chances.

Hispanic sonnet, or Tongue-tied

John of Patmos meant
Poetry is the tongue of God.
Kierkegaard meant
Poetry is soaring over the world.
I am no less unshackled nor
Heavenlier despite these words—
Enticing symbols
Despite their flaws.
Love yourself & asylum what is
Weak—bodies' fragile
Collapsing.
University taught me to
Talk smack about universities.
God handed me vocabulary to

Tongue-tie my soul.

Hispanic sonnet, or Crazy veins

I'm loyal to my hunger like a dog.
Like a dog I'm loyal to my masters.
I'm master of none like Aziz Ansari.
Like Aziz Ansari I play to the crowds.
I'm crowded spiritually like a lapsed Marxist.
Like a lapsed Marxist I turn to love.
I'm in love with the sound of turning pages.
Like turning pages I'm qualified to slice skin.
I'm a grid of sliced skin like Pinhead.
Like Pinhead I'm an adversary of the sun.
I'm the sun in a body as one of many-bodied sons.
Like an obedient son I'm cursed with Catholic guilt.
I'm guilty of the sin of sheltering crazy veins.
Like veins my walls are wafers against chaos.

I'm of the belief that chaos is boogeyman of words.

Hispanic sonnet, or Running gag

Somewhere sacred & quiet & a
Buzz screams across the silence &
I turn around to spot a fly trapped
Behind windowsills—specifically
Behind a wood carving of the Last
Supper. There's a running gag to be
Found here, muses I. But no. Locked
Inside this Hispanic sonnet is a deathly-
Serious matter at large. What it is,
Can't quite specify. Give me time
On that. Am one bitter cup of joe
Into today & already I suspect I'm a
Half man with half-man rationale.
Which begs the obvious question:

Why haven't I freed the fly already?

Hispanic sonnet, or Woman's work

Came out
Like a bullet—
No, like a boulder
In molasses—jaundiced &
Cone-headed with a patch of
Mossy hair & shortly I amassed
Hot Wheels & Civil War chronicles
Scavenged from garage sales & night
After night catapulted Spaldings on driveways
Dreaming buzzer beaters & mansion shopping &
Backne arrived just in time to wave the cooties off &
My high school crush stomped me a new chest cavity
And later I juggled three hearts & discovered I wasn't cut
For the circus. Poetry swooped in, ruptured my jugular. Dracula.

Mother showed me raising a man is woman's work.

Hispanic sonnet, or Invisible wire

I tell kids, I say, You don't write to change
The world, you write to change yourself.
Occasionally I wish upon them the wasp-sting of
200 rejections. Occasionally I'm mean-spirited
As such. But after 200 nos, 200 unfortunatelys,
I'm adeptly immune to the consequences of wrong
Words for the wrong magazines. That's all it is:
Semantics. The dance of matching your flavors with
Other plausible tastebuds. This last clause I must rephrase
Into a pertinent, politically correct message for kids.
So many people would rather play it safe.
From the comfort of my sofa, these lines land on
This page safely. If I'm being candid, I'd surmise I've

Played it as safe as anybody straddling an invisible wire.

Hispanic sonnet, or Snowdrift

If I were a cat, wouldn't be here to
Tell you I'm not a cat. A feral cat
Slumbers in my front porch—
White-gray face, huge human-blue
Eyes, chunk of forehead missing
Following a catfight. My neighbors
Feed him, I don't, but we respect
Each other, me & Mr. Cat.
Haven't a clue what they've
Named him. In a cookbook my
Mom inherited from the 1920s
Flour is referred to as snowdrift.
You're thinking, Call the cat Snowdrift.
You're thinking, Feed Snowdrift!

Snowdrift's overweight. He naps on a bed of leaves.

Hispanic sonnet, or Burning the midnight oil

In my mind I'm always writing from
The center of Earth, which is to say,
The most horrifying place in the
World. In my mind I always write
From the core of my heart which I
Firmly believe will shut off the
Blood in 34 more years. In my mind
I'm not a vampire but a shadow of
A castle wall that'll crumble upon a
Peck from a butterfly. When I was a
Boy I believed the oil refinery past
The cottonfield was a fiery metropolis
Governed by a fanged count. My
Father—a persuasive storyteller.

There, fire still scorches the night sky.

Hispanic sonnet, or The burbs

Back then, past insanity's doors. At a New Year's party
Smoked a Cuban cigar with a retired elevator
Mechanic who not a year later slashed his throat
In his backyard. His wife worked for the
Chicago Blackhawks, flashed a championship
Ring the size of a humble penthouse. Their
Porchlights from mid-century basked us in primary
Colors. Fireflies burned in oblivion. The man
Left me a pit-stained undershirt he'd worn to cheer
Da Bears. Was reading *Pet Sematary* when I
Heard the news & knew the city was an oven &
Evil convalesced in the burbs. This isn't a
Metaphor for Hell on Earth. This isn't a South
Texas ghost story. It's a PSA: Retirees, we

Admire you so. If you need an ear, hugs, just ask.

Hispanic sonnet, or Saturday afternoon

The difference between me & my bundle of
Records is when the needle scratches them
They bathe my living room in gorgeous
Music. Eek. This is the inverse of magical
Thinking. Don't use needles like that.
Maintain a clean lifestyle. I'm like a retired
Wrestler who went vegan minus the no
Eating fast food. I'm in a mood. It's Saturday
Afternoon & the toxic couple three units
Down is officially dissolved. My head's
Bloated with Morgan Parker poems about
Beyoncé & the decision I'll have to make
Someday when, where & if to baptize my
Child. At this juncture, I'm without child.

Destiny's child. Destiny, what's my next play?

Hispanic sonnet, or Spiritual diversion

A couple few times in church I recall
Hankering chicken tenders leading up to
Holy Communion. When asked when did
I more or less accept Christ as Lord &
Savior, I usually reply the age I am. Have
Made the best breakthroughs during meals.
Made the worst breakthroughs during
Meals. Poetry's proudly suited for
Spiritual diversion. There's something
Wholly unappetizing about Jesus-sized
Gruesome crucifixes. Have always wondered
How many other pairs of eyes are distracted
By agony above the pulpit. It's weird cultures
We're groomed in. Stomachs speak truths.

Tongues are vipers charmed with lies.

Hispanic sonnet, or The shape of sound at prayer's end

Take it from me: goading a young buck to
Taste Arby's Horsey Sauce should come
With a disclaimer: this packaged
Whiteness, my dear child, is grossly unlike
Grandma's vanilla pudding. We joke
My dad's side of the family relishes
In the physical misery of others.
Minor blunders, usually: a man racked
On a log, a dog tripping a newlywedded
Bride. America's Funniest Home Videos
Type garbage. This poem's anti-elegant &
It's bothering me something ugly. 'Tis
The season for forgiveness. Sin's year
Round. Round's the shape of Anglo

Mouths blooming, "Amen, amen, amen."

Hispanic sonnet, or Ode to Manu Ginóbili (or Credit to our kind)

If John Wayne devoted majority screen time erasing
Indians & Schwarzenegger blasting blanks, browns,
Whites & other assorted predators, why not give it
Up for Emanuel David Ginóbili—El Contusion.
Olympian, expunger of Perón. At 15, when I came of age
On the blacktop, they called me Manu. Pale-skinned,
Black-maned, floppy arms attached to dagger 'bows,
I shot, Euro-drove, dished & it was always, "Manu!
Manu! Yo, who guardin' that mouse Manu?" Man, that
Shit. My shame unfathomably deep. Latin. But like a
Myth, many rotations later & it's a blessing I can praise on
Behalf of little-big-city San Antone, but chiefly
Myself—diced-onion shots missed & swished, tears of
Tabasco: Thank you, Manu. Thank you, Manu. Thank u,

Gracias. May you remain my saint this mortal life deserves.

Hispanic sonnet, or Facemask

So we're clear, a face is a
Facemask.
What's the longest you've gone with a
Soiled facemask?
What's the longest you've gone with no one
Around to aim your
Facemask at?
Approximately every two new moons I trim my
Facemask.
Consider my severed beard hairs a mass of
Facemasked bandits.
Some folks possess unwavering
Faith in the notion of trustworthy
Blockading of critical holes on

Facemasks, born double agents, like hellacious poems.

Hispanic sonnet, or Casual fan

Take my heart &
My feet stamp the
Trampled path. Seize
My books and I pursue
You into the borderless
Void. The cost of doing
Business w/ these words is
Burning skin from the
Inside out. The price of
Life hopping labels is
Ducking gunshots disrupting
My homespun jazz. There's a
Mexican standoff in my
Head. Peacemakers fully

Loaded. I root for both sides.

Hispanic sonnet, or White names

A Black off-duty policeman told me,
"We christened our children White
Names so they'll have equal chance."
Wanted to ask him, But what happens
After the big reveal? Wanted to tell him,
But sir, the fickle gods will not save them.
Wanted to say, Word up, officer, that's
Foolproof strategy. Me, I nodded &
Smiled. If you grew up fond of your
Name, perhaps this poem isn't for you.
Perhaps on scientific levels everything's
Connected & a most utopian expression
Remains: all-inclusive. As in: if we each
Die alone, loneliness is all-inclusive. As in:

Handcuffs without hands. As in: these names are still too tight.

Hispanic sonnet, or Ars poetica

Maybe it starts with being born.
Bodies stretch with words.
Overflow kills or rewards.
In small ways, slow time.
In no time much said, much lost.
Do bodies expend all they can?
On this chair, at my table, I'm relevant.
Inside this shell, in bed, I'm an animal.
I bloat with surplus syllables.
Have they made homes of my bones?
Was born & made a mess.
Will die & make a mess.
Dirt is older than dirt.
My unspent words sprout another body &

I hardly recognize the doppelgänger.

Hispanic sonnet, or Oscar Zeta Acosta's spirit gritos during Hispanic Heritage Month

Watch
     Me
          Roam
Hear
     Me
          ROAR
I'm
     Drug
          Psycho
& pistol
     Sharp
          Brown
Buffalos
     Never

Vanish / El Dorado in the clouds.

Hispanic sonnet, or Punk sensibility

Chicano poetry necessitates punk sensibility.
"Necessitate" is a word choice professors may
Respect. The distinction between primary &
Higher education is critical thinking & diction.
Diction—try out this word at a party. Electrify the
Ladies. Wink wink. Guys, Irish painter Francis
Bacon revered venerable masters so mightily he
Snatched their frameworks & muddied 'em.
Chicano poetry necessitates destructive flair.
I'm truly scared to detonate how I really want to.
Scared I'll explode in a million directions &
The shards will hint of Mexican dark chocolate.
If you make a show of reciting poems to every
Mirror, you're ripe for the big leagues. Right as a

Bent [insert noun]. I hate punk rock, therefore am punk.

Hispanic sonnet, or Adornment

I dreamt I was the sword of
Don Quixote & a fly landed
On my tip & proclaimed
I, Sancho Panza, relieve thee of
Duty, & I was incensed yet also
Flushed at the vainglory &
Valor of the fly to distinguish
In me an accessory whose
Vocation was purely to adorn his
Foolish hero & I wept tears of
Springwater & nourished the
Undulating Spanish countryside &
Carnations smoothed my brittle
Nerves & I woke to a chorus of

Windmills fanning in unity.

Hispanic sonnet, or Unquiet mind

I dreamt of an unquiet mind
A body of work
A crow named Jim perched on
Percival Everett's shoulder
Poultry of creation
Casualty of poetry
Audacity of
Ethics
Amnesia's zeitgeist
Entropy's whitewash
Old age's blackouts
Rash of blistering suns
Preeminence of breath
Bracing salve of mud, ah

Chasm withstanding.

Hispanic sonnet, or Had a dream

Had a dream this nation rose up & lived out
The true meaning of its creed & my little
Children were not judged by the colors of their
Skins but by the contents of their characters &
After I purchased the last two chocolate
Frosted donuts at Shipley's, American Express
Charged me $10 for not spending a minimum of
$10—regardless, I was cavalier & in this inclination
Forked over my receipt to my financial adviser who
Rebuked me on my failure to be prudent—I asked
Her, Do you even know what prudence means? &
She answered, Of course, my livelihood depends on
It, & I rebutted, If you're preoccupied with prudence
Then why haven't you rehabilitated my abysmal diet?

Buried in secondary definitions—can you hear me scream?

Hispanic sonnet, or The logic of magic

There're two kinds of folks: those who deem
Their bodies their own & those who're extra with
Sharing. Just cuz a poem teaches one how to
Read it doesn't mean it's to be trusted. I watch my
Back against turned backs. For whom the bell tolls
Are those who listen. For whom the world's a sight to
Behold are those who watch. Believe it or not, un-
Predictability's a kind of delicate logic.
The logic of magic is such that if you've ever
Uttered the word "vibe," you're a magician.
The space between east & west is a central
Conundrum. I leak words like Zeno's arrows &
Their meanings never reach you. If a phone rings &
Nobody picks up, you're wedged in the matrix.

If you squint hard, whoa, I almost look like Keanu Reeves.

Hispanic sonnet, or '90s kid (or Guilty pleasure)

hot as h-e-double hockey sticks outside
even if it were 98 degrees cooler (as if)
but this totally means it'll be an evening of
passion & O! Ace of Base straight radio sprayin'
"All That She Wants" i lip-sync like a mofo
(whatever batman 4ever i don't care) / the
mise-en-scène was tight & i w/ home skillets
2 kool 4 blue's clues but not the shallow end of the
skool pool where Mr. Pascal (RIP) gifted us underwater
wings / stopped drop dead fred under the bridge / worn
woman rappin' my window for support—some
thankless cause or another—not it!—the second i
accelerate i slam into those sagging eyes & i got
the city blues bad / *all that she wants is another baby*

tomorrow i'm gone / then baby (oh no) i'm back.

Hispanic sonnet, or Dark heart

Like a cluster of electrons I'm chronically unreliable.
I'm like a chronic case of basic bitch.
Like a cold case file I crave warm touch.
I'm like a touch of functional & that's it.
Like a quadratic function I'm two degrees from my Maker.
I'm not like the Holy Ghost in various degrees.
Like variability I roll off the tongue roughly.
I'm like a hood tongue in need of saving.
Like an aimless tongue I pave paths in spit.
I'm like a split path casting dual shadows.
Like a shadow I'm a branch of my name.
I'm merely a name like everybody else.
Like everybody else I'm a collection of veins.
I'm like a vein pumping a dark heart.

Like a dark heart I weep when nobody's around.

Hispanic sonnet, or Outside my walls

To be so happy to be levitated out of time
A smile presented freely I take wherever comes next
Everywhere probing for God
Most nights falling on sleep
Flesh stockpiling ordinary time few stunning words may leak
Shakespeare collapses against the apocalypse
Balanced smiles beg asymmetry
Curved tongues twisting wills of words
A miracle steering straight in the maze of my mind
Show the way, pure people
For goodness like enchantment
A cloud straddled as the last buffalo on the plains
Circle back & genuflect before the altar of disappointment
Mathematics can't justify the shrieking women outside my walls

Eye of my body—preservation & mercy—please, call my bluff.

Hispanic sonnet, or American dream

They'd assigned me to outfield. Squatted, gloved
Arm raised toward heaven, eyes glazed over the
Diamond, I waited for contact that never arrived.
Like Borges' circular man, I lived the dream of
A wizard who stitched me from nothing. Like
All dreams, mine was nebulous & real.
Stars & stripes. Behaved in school, I dodged
Whips, tied my tongue in kennels. In sunlight
They stuffed my face with books. In moonlight
I dumped it all in static tubes. Dreamt reveries of
A nameless conjurer. From university I flew to
Metropolis where bodies swan dive onto
Concrete. Openings. Closings. Music nonstop.
Cups in hand, some of us waltz into gleaming

Bayonets. We're better than our fathers, so said the father.

Hispanic sonnet, or Pretend to understand

Sweet girl, I tell you
Everything's gonna be okay
I've got a rotten feeling we're after
The same thing
Reserve your love notes for yourself
Your body beneath skin
Shovel the rest up to roving clouds
Poetry like the moon glows only when you see it
Resides in your eyes when it floats away—
The sun's out
Tap tap tap my nasal bridge
Let's compare dreams on a picnic blanket
Name each ant like an army of children under
A livable sky we didn't ask for &

Pretend to understand.

Hispanic sonnet, or End of American maniac

for David Spicer

David, you're dying / but it feels as tho
You've written yourself out of death.
Sestina King, American Maniac, your
Mind let go but the machines keep you
Breathing. For now. Not much longer.
Remember you told me how in 1980
You accompanied Denis Johnson to an
Arizona prison to visit a mutual friend? You
Said Denis was a marvelous man & writer
And minutes later that Hollywood'll fuck
Anything up, Shelley's *Frankenstein* as
Proof. You blurbed I had cojones to publish
Poems about God. Naw. David, I have to
Tell you, before goodbye, grab the nearest

Partner. Dance. This life. Unbearably sad. Precious.

About the Author

Alex Z. Salinas is the author of four poetry collections and a book of stories, *City Lights From the Upside Down*, which was included in the National Book Critics Circle's Critical Notes. He holds an M.A. in English Literature and Language from St. Mary's University, and lives in San Antonio, Texas.

FLOWERSONG
P R E S S

FlowerSong Press nurtures essential verse
from, about, and throughout the
borderlands. Literary. Lyrical. Boundless.

Sign up for announcements about
new and upcoming titles at:

www.flowersongpress.com

Printed in the USA
CPSIA information can be obtained
at www.ICGtesting.com
LVHW031110060124
767849LV00024B/467